PAKISTANIS IN AMERICA

web enhanced at www.inamericabooks.com

STACY TAUS-BOLSTAD

LERNER PUBLICATIONS COMPANY / MINNEAPOLIS

Current information and statistics quickly become out of date. That's why we developed **www.inamericabooks.com**, a companion website to the **In America** series. The site offers lots of additional information—downloadable photos and maps and up-to-date facts through links to additional websites. Each link has been carefully selected by researchers at Lerner Publishing Group and is regularly reviewed and updated. However, Lerner Publishing Group is not responsible for the accuracy or suitability of material on websites that are not maintained directly by us. It is recommended that students using the Internet be supervised by a parent, a librarian, a teacher, or another adult.

Lerner Publications Company
A division of Lerner Publishing Group
241 First Avenue North
Minneapolis, MN 55401 U.S.A.

Website address: www.lernerbooks.com

Library of Congress Cataloging-in-Publication Data

Taus-Bolstad, Stacy.
    Pakistanis in America / by Stacy Taus-Bolstad.
        p.   cm. — (In America)
    Includes bibliographical references and index.
    ISBN-13: 978-0-8225-4872-0 (lib. bdg. : alk. paper)
    ISBN-10: 0-8225-4872-0 (lib. bdg. : alk. paper)
    1. Pakistani Americans–History–Juvenile literature. 2. Pakistani Americans–Juvenile literature. 3. Immigrants–United States–Juvenile literature. I. Title. II. Series: In America (Minneapolis, Minn.)
    E184.P28T38 2006
    973'.04914122–dc22   2005010235

Manufactured in the United States of America
1 2 3 4 5 6 – JR – 11 10 09 08 07 06

CONTENTS

INTRODUCTION

In America, a walk down a city street can seem like a walk through many lands. Grocery stores sell international foods. Shops offer products from around the world. People strolling past may speak foreign languages. This unique blend of cultures is the result of America's history as a nation of immigrants.

Native peoples have lived in North America for centuries. The next settlers were the Vikings. In about A.D. 1000, they sailed from Scandinavia to lands that would become Canada, Greenland, and Iceland. In 1492 the Italian navigator Christopher Columbus landed in the Americas, and more European explorers arrived during the 1500s. In the 1600s, British settlers formed colonies that, after the Revolutionary War (1775–1783), would become the United States. And in the mid-1800s, a great wave of immigration brought millions of new arrivals to the young country.

Immigrants have many different reasons for leaving home. They may leave to escape poverty, war, or harsh governments. They may want better living conditions for themselves and their children. Throughout its history, America has been known as a nation that offers many opportunities. For this reason, many immigrants come to America.

Moving to a new country is not easy. It can mean making a long, difficult journey. It means leaving home and starting over in an unfamiliar place. But it also means using skill, talent, and determination to build a new life. The In America series tells the story of immigration to the United States and the search for fresh beginnings in a new country—in America.

PAKISTANIS IN AMERICA

Pakistanis are a relatively new immigrant group to America. Because Pakistan was not independent until 1947, the number of Pakistani immigrants was not recorded until that year. But people from the Indian subcontinent (a region in southern Asia that includes modern-day India, Pakistan, and Bangladesh) began moving to the United States in the late 1800s. For these early settlers, America meant freedom from the poverty and harsh government that dominated their lives on the subcontinent.

Even after Pakistan won its independence in 1947, poverty and ethnic violence plagued the young nation. Many wanted to seek opportunities in other lands, including America. Restrictive laws kept Pakistani immigration to a trickle at first, but when these laws were lifted in 1965, the trickle became a flood. The Pakistani American community boomed, becoming one of America's fastest-growing and most dynamic ethnic groups. In 2005 an estimated two hundred thousand people of Pakistani descent lived in the United States. But census estimates may not accurately reflect the Pakistani American population, due to wording and categories on census questionnaires. Some questionnaires group Pakistanis with other Asians, making it difficult to know the actual number of Pakistanis in America.

Pakistani Americans have made important contributions to American society. They are doctors, teachers, students, and businesspeople. At times, they have struggled with prejudice and discrimination—especially following the September 11, 2001, terrorist attacks on the United States. But through determination and hard work, Pakistani Americans have created a rich and vibrant community, bridging the gap between their Pakistani heritage and their American home.

1 LIFE ON THE SUBCONTINENT

Pakistan covers about three hundred thousand square miles of the Indian subcontinent in southern Asia. China shares Pakistan's northeastern border, and the country of Afghanistan lies to the northwest and west of Pakistan. To the south sits the Arabian Sea, and Iran stretches along Pakistan's southwestern border. India is Pakistan's eastern neighbor. Pakistan's capital city is Islamabad.

Pakistan's geography includes some of the most mountainous terrain in the world, particularly the Northern Areas and the North–West Frontier Province. In southern Pakistan, the Indus River divides the country into two regions. In the east lies the fertile Indus River valley, which includes Sindh and Punjab provinces. West of the Indus River rises the Baluchistan Plateau and the province of Baluchistan. Farther south, the valley becomes drier, eventually turning into the Thar Desert.

Soaring mountains, fertile valleys, and arid deserts all characterize Pakistan's landscape. These geographic differences, coupled with little rainfall, cause temperature extremes. Cold weather hits most of the country from December to March, and temperatures often drop below freezing at this time. The hot season, with temperatures soaring well above 100°F, lasts from April to June. In July monsoons (heavy rain–bearing winds) arrive, making the warm air humid and sticky. The wet season lasts until September. October and November are usually the most comfortable months in Pakistan.

Terraced farms flank the Indus River in northern Pakistan. The river valley is a rich agricultural area in an otherwise arid (dry) country.

Because this diverse topography and extreme climate often made travel difficult, wide ethnic and regional differences have developed. Most people choose to follow their own local customs. They usually speak their regional language instead of the official national language, Urdu. For example, people living in the Sindh Province speak Sindhi, while people in the neighboring Punjab region speak Punjabi. People often think of themselves in terms of their regional identity, rather than as Pakistanis. These language and ethnic barriers have largely kept the people of Pakistan from creating a solid national identity.

EARLY HISTORY

While Pakistan is a young nation, the land is steeped in such a long and rich history that the region is sometimes called the Cradle of Civilization. One of the region's earliest societies began about 2500 B.C. near the Indus River and expanded into the area that became Pakistan. The ancient Indus civilization flourished until about 1700 B.C.

Around the same time, a group of people called Aryans, who originated in central Asia, took control of the northern regions of the Indian subcontinent. The Aryans followed a religion called Hinduism, which featured many gods and goddesses.

A main component of Aryan society was the caste system, a rigid class structure that defined people's jobs, family life, and society. Hindus (followers of Hinduism) believed in reincarnation, the idea that a person's soul does not die but passes from one life to another. It was thought that whatever caste a person was born into was the result of the person's past life. If a person lived a good life, he or she might be born into a higher caste in the next life.

The Aryans remained in power for about one thousand years. During this time, they expanded their realm across the northern half of the subcontinent. But smaller political units within the Aryan territory also arose. By the A.D. 600s, these Aryan clans and kingdoms were fighting for control of the subcontinent.

Meanwhile, on the Arabian Peninsula in the Middle East, the prophet Muhammad was founding a new religion called Islam. Muslims (followers of Islam) believed in one god, Allah, whose teachings were collected in Islam's sacred book, the Quran.

The Quran (below), *Islam's holy book, is written in Arabic. Muslims consider the Quran to be the word of Allah himself and believe the book to be a copy of an eternal book kept in heaven.*

When Muhammad died in A.D. 632, his followers began to spread their religion to new lands. Muslim traders, who conducted business along the Arabian Sea coastline, soon introduced their religion to the Indian subcontinent.

Hindus and Muslims faced enormous cultural and religious differences. One of the biggest differences between these two groups stemmed from some of their most basic beliefs. Hinduism is polytheistic, meaning its followers believe in many gods and goddesses. Islam, on the other hand, teaches that Allah is the one supreme god. Another important difference is in the social system. Hindus follow the rigid caste system, but Muslims believe all men are equal in the eyes of Allah.

THE FIVE PILLARS OF ISLAM

Muslims follow five basic duties, called pillars, set forth in the Quran. These duties are:

- Believing in Allah and the prophet Muhammad
- Praying five times every day
- Giving to the poor
- Fasting during the holy month of Ramadan
- Attempting to make the hajj *(right)*, a pilgrimage to Mecca in Saudi Arabia (the birthplace of the prophet Muhammad)

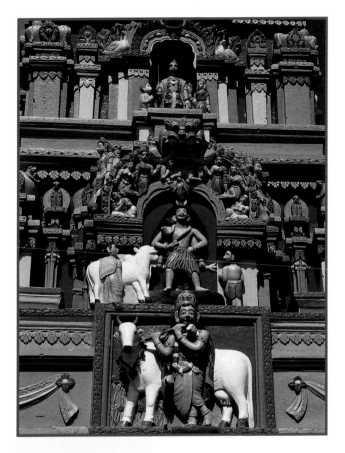

The gods Shiva (center) *and Krishna* (bottom), *among others, decorate this Hindu temple in India.*

Religious and cultural beliefs became a source of tension between the two groups. For example, Hindu temples were decorated with images of gods and goddesses. Islam, however, forbids artists to depict human figures. Muslims considered these Hindu images disrespectful. Equally offensive to Hindus was the fact that Muslims butchered and ate cows, which Hindus consider sacred animals.

In addition to differences between Hindus and Muslims, different customs and beliefs exist among the followers of Islam. Two major sects of Islam are the Sunnis and the Shiites. One of the biggest differences between the two is the question of Muhammad's successor. Sunnis believe that Muhammad's successor could be a wise colleague, while Shiites believe that only a blood relative could succeed him. These differences—which date back to Islam's early years—dictate the customs and beliefs of their followers and are often a source of political tension. At times, they have led to violence between sects.

Despite all of these differences, the new faith spread peacefully on the subcontinent at first. Islam was especially appealing to many Hindus at the bottom of the caste system, because it did not include the strict social structure of Hinduism.

To learn more about Hinduism and Islam, visit WWW.INAMERICABOOKS.COM for links.

At the beginning of the eleventh century, however, Islamic tribes from the area that eventually became Turkey began invading the subcontinent. Seeking to expand their empire, these Turkish-speaking people launched attacks on Hindu settlements. When they met resistance, they responded with violence, usually killing rebels and destroying Hindu temples. Conquered people were sometimes given a choice between death or converting to Islam. Harsh laws were also established for non-Muslim subjects, including heavy taxes and restricted political power.

In the following century, Islam gained more converts as Muslim leaders conquered new territory. By the late 1100s, a Muslim kingdom called the Delhi Sultanate was in place at Delhi, India. The sultanate lasted until 1526, when Mongol forces from central Asia conquered the northern subcontinent and set up the Mughal Empire.

Although the Mongols were Muslims, many Mughal rulers tolerated Hinduism, and the two religions coexisted. For the most part, Muslim and Hindu communities lived side by side. They conducted their business in peace, and some even intermarried.

European Influences

In the 1500s, European explorers and merchants began to see the subcontinent as a valuable region for trade. Britain, France, the Netherlands, and Portugal soon began competing for Mughal goods.

By the 1600s, a British organization known as the East India Company had established the first permanent European colony (foreign settlement) in India. The company dabbled in everything from teas and spices to fabrics and jewelry. This early settlement served as a trading station, allowing Britain to import and export goods at a lower cost. It also helped the British gain a foothold in the subcontinent's culture.

These early British settlers lived very much like most locals. Company employees learned Indian customs and languages. They often married Indian women and started families. These personal connections eventually gave the British a strong advantage over other European powers, who began fighting one another for trading rights in India in the 1700s. But by this time, the British East India Company had already emerged as the Mughal Empire's most important trading partner. And the company continued to expand, setting up offices in India's ports. Company agents usually tried to make peaceful agreements with local rulers as they extended British influence. But when they did encounter resistance, especially as they progressed inland, they used violence and force to defeat it. To battle local resistance as well as foreign rivals, the British maintained a strong military presence on the subcontinent.

To add to British troops, the company employed sepoys—Indian soldiers trained and led by European officers. While sepoys were originally hired to protect the company's trading interests, local rulers often sought their services to resolve regional strife. Such unrest had grown in recent years as the Mughal Empire itself had begun to decline. The emperor Aurangzeb, who ruled until 1707, had used up much of the realm's resources trying to expand his territory. In addition, Aurangzeb was a strict Muslim who alienated many of his Hindu subjects by destroying their temples and by passing laws that discriminated against them. These internal problems badly weakened the empire, making its people more willing to offer the British trading privileges and cooperation in return for military assistance.

The East India Company's efforts were rewarded in 1717 when the Mughal emperor granted the British control over thirty-eight villages near the city of Calcutta. This area became the headquarters of British colonial administration on the subcontinent, and its central factories and administrative buildings became known as "White Town."

Firmly established in the region, the company began playing a larger political role. Through the 1700s and the 1800s, it absorbed independent regions throughout the subcontinent—including areas that would later become part of Pakistan. The company also used its political and military power to demand taxes from locals and even passed a law allowing Britain to take over the fortunes of Indian princes who died without heirs. And to prevent local groups from uniting against British control, officials took advantage of rivalries

To become emperor, Aurangzeb (on throne, above) *defeated three of his brothers and imprisoned his father.*

between different rulers, religions, and social classes in the region.

As Britain expanded its territory and its influence on the subcontinent, its colonists also began to westernize India. (*Western* is a geographic and political term usually used to refer to the culture and history of the United States and Europe.) They introduced European technology, ideas, and habits, and wanted local peoples to follow their rules. The British, who followed the Christian religion, viewed Hindu and Islamic beliefs as barbaric, and the British stifled local customs and religious practices. As more and more British citizens settled in India, they became less willing to adapt to local ways. Many British colonists knew nothing about the region's culture or customs and tended to consider locals inferior. This attitude created a huge rift between the British and the Indians—both Muslims and Hindus.

By 1854 the British claimed authority over most of modern-day Pakistan and a large part of India. Many people of the subcontinent were not happy with this foreign occupation. The company used the subcontinent's natural resources for its own wealth. Indian leaders watched British merchants grow richer, while local people became poorer. They also disliked the high taxes that the British demanded and the lack of power that regional rulers had.

Decades of resentment over British economic and social policies exploded in 1857 when Indian soldiers of the British Indian Army, particularly from the army's Muslim units, rebelled against the British. This uprising was called the Sepoy Rebellion.

The bloody yearlong civil war that followed seriously threatened British control in India and wreaked havoc on both the local population and on British forces. But the revolt was ill-planned, and many Indian princes supported the British in the hopes that European powers would grant them political favors after the war. British soldiers defeated the last of the rebels in 1858.

The damage from the revolt was deep. Bitter resentment and distrust remained on both sides. The British especially blamed Muslims, who were believed to have had a major role in planning and leading the revolt. As a result, many Muslims were labeled as traitors and publicly executed.

Though the Sepoy Rebellion in 1857 was largely unsuccessful, sepoys did capture several major cities, including Delhi. The battle for Delhi is depicted in the illustration above.

THE SEPOY REBELLION

A rumor may have sparked the Sepoy Rebellion of 1857. It was believed that the gunpowder cartridges that the army used were greased with the fat of hogs and cows. When Indian soldiers were commanded to bite into these cartridges during battle in order to load their guns, neither group was willing to do so. (Muslims consider hogs unclean, and cows are sacred animals to Hindus.) The order was the final insult to the Indian sepoys, who had grown tired of fighting for their repressive British administrators.

To learn more about the Sepoy Rebellion and British rule in India, visit www.inamericabooks.com for links.

Soon after the war, Britain's government decided that the East India Company could not effectively rule India. The British government officially took over the rule of India in 1858.

LIFE UNDER BRITISH RULE

The British government appointed an official called a viceroy (also known as the governor-general) to rule India. The viceroy was aided by other officials spread about the region. This system was known as the Indian Civil Service, but only British-born officials could serve in this administration. They received high salaries and status, while Indian leaders were all but excluded from the service.

However, to maintain control of such a large and diverse area, Britain needed the help of local leaders. They gained this support by promising local princes that they would still be allowed to govern their states—as long as they agreed to answer to British administrators. This policy angered many people, who felt that their leaders had sold out.

Under British rule, the people of the subcontinent did see some important advancements. The British government began improving India's economy by encouraging large-scale industry, including manufacturing and mining, and by expanding trade. Massive irrigation (watering) projects increased agricultural production. A railway network was established to link important cities and to provide a better transportation system for people and goods. Communications systems were set up, including telegraph and telephone lines. India was soon called the crown jewel of the British Empire.

British colonization also brought some social changes, especially for women. Measures were taken to stop the custom of suttee, in which a wife was expected to commit suicide after her husband's death. Girls and women could also receive basic schooling, which had been almost unheard of before the British invasion.

However, nearly all of the changes the British made in India were done for the good of the East India Company, not the good of the local people. Most public works—developments such as better hospitals, better housing in the cities, and better access to clean water and adequate food supplies, which would have significantly improved average people's living conditions—were ignored.

Some British reforms actually hurt the residents of the subcontinent. For example, the government combined small family-owned farms into plantations (large estates), forcing poor farmers to sell their land to the government. Many were left completely homeless and unable to feed themselves. Huge numbers of rural families left the countryside and the only homes most of them had ever known, resettling in urban areas to find jobs in newly opened factories.

These factories presented problems of their own. Factory workers mass-produced goods such as textiles and handicrafts, leaving small-scale artisans struggling to compete. Millions of weavers, potters, metalworkers, and other craftspeople found themselves unable to make a living at the handicrafts that had sustained their families for centuries.

As British India's people became poorer, they also grew more isolated. Most British officials and their families, considering the people of the subcontinent inferior to themselves, lived in areas set apart from Indian communities. Private clubs allowed the British to socialize exclusively, keeping the native population at a distance.

While the British government dominated Indian politics, economy, and society, it had promised to stay out of the region's religious affairs. Most of the people of British India followed Hinduism. Muslims made up the second-largest group, although their numbers remained fairly small compared to the Hindu population.

Nevertheless, colonial administrators used religious and cultural differences to divide Hindus and Muslims. When dealing with Hindu leaders, British governors blamed the Muslim population for problems and vice versa. Keeping the two groups from uniting against them allowed Britain to maintain firmer control over the subcontinent and its varied groups. But fighting among Muslims, Hindus, and British colonials began to plague the area.

In addition, Hindus and Muslims were forbidden to rise higher than low-ranking office positions in the complex British system of government administration and law. They were not allowed to participate in upper-level military positions.

We have maintained our power in India by playing-off one part against the other, and we must continue to do so. Do all you can, therefore, to prevent all having a common feeling.

—Lord Salisbury (secretary of state for India) to Lord Elgin (viceroy), 1862

Muslims especially lost many rights under their British rulers. The British believed that Christianity was superior to Islam, which they regarded as a rigid and primitive religion. One governor even passed an order stating that Muslims should not rise above the level of ink fillers. The people no longer had a voice in their own land.

The feeling of inequality for Muslims was heightened when Britain closed India's village schools and made the English language required in city schools. Some Islamic leaders believed that going to European-run schools was a good way for the Muslim minority to succeed socially and politically under colonial rule. Overall, however, most Muslims insisted on attending their own schools. Muslim leaders viewed the British occupation as not only a religious clash but also as a clash of civilizations, and they saw their traditional schools as a way of protecting both their religion and their culture. But

A group of young boys attend an outdoor class at a traditional Muslim school in India. Although these schools faced challenges during the years of British rule, they survived and remain important in modern Pakistan and India.

without government support or resources, enrollment at these schools was often limited to wealthier families.

Children of the most prominent Indian families were encouraged to study abroad at British schools. Britain hoped that this would create an educated Indian elite that would feel loyal to the British government. But Indians who went to school abroad found themselves in an undesirable position when they returned to the subcontinent. Despite their education and loyalty, they were still unable to move ahead. Political positions were given only to British-born officials. At the same time, the years that British-educated Indians spent abroad left them with little understanding of their own country and culture.

SIR SYED

Sir Syed Ahmad Khan (1817–1898) was a scholar and Muslim leader who urged Muslims living under British rule to learn as much about Western culture as they could. He was especially interested in European scientific ideas and believed that Islamic education should adapt to these more modern ideas. He also hoped that gaining an understanding of European education and politics would help Muslim leaders bridge the cultural gap between these two groups. His efforts succeeded in generating interest in Western knowledge, and he eventually established the Aligarh Muslim University in Aligarh, India. This institution promoted understanding between Muslims and the British, while also supporting the central ideas of Islamic teaching.

They often came home practicing European habits, dressing in European clothing, and following European customs. They were not accepted by the native population, yet they were not considered equals by the British. They felt adrift in their homeland.

MAKING CHANGES

Under British rule, life for most people of the subcontinent had steadily declined. Farmers had lost their land. Families could not make enough money to survive. People living in India's overcrowded cities faced starvation. Many were homeless.

More and more people wanted to be free of British rule. As Britain became aware of growing unrest, the government took harsher measures. For example, it introduced the Rowlatt Act. Under this law, a person could be arrested for owning a scrap of writing that advocated freedom for India.

In 1885 local leaders opposed to the British occupation officially banded together to form the Indian National Congress. This group demanded independence for India.

At first, Muslims supported the congress. Muslim leader Mohammed Ali Jinnah in particular supported Hindu–Muslim cooperation. He believed Hindus and Muslims could live peacefully together under a united and independent India. It wasn't long, however, before Islamic leaders began to think that India's Muslim minority was not adequately represented by the congress. Fearing that the Hindu majority would never allow Muslims to have any significant political power, they believed that they needed their own political voice.

In the meantime, other pressing problems arose. In the last years of the 1800s, famine (a severe food shortage) ravaged the subcontinent. The crisis further aggravated tensions among the British, Muslims, and Hindus as each group blamed the others. Food supplies dwindled, livestock died, and families faced starvation. Thousands died, and the future looked bleaker than ever.

2 MOVING TO AMERICA

As conditions on the subcontinent worsened in the late 1800s and early 1900s, large numbers of people first began leaving for America. The majority of these immigrants were Sikhs. A minority religious group, Sikhs formed less than 2 percent of the subcontinent's total population. They hailed from the Punjab, a northwestern region that was later divided between India and Pakistan. The Sikh religion (established in the 1400s) combines certain parts of Hinduism and Islam. Sikhs' holy book, the Granth, is dedicated to unity, truth, and one god.

A small group of Punjabi Muslims also moved to the United States in the late 1800s and early 1900s. The majority of Sikhs and Punjabi Muslims were farmers. As drought (water shortages) ruined their lands, many Punjabi men left India to find work, leaving their wives and children behind. They hoped to make enough money to support their starving families. America—where farms prospered and wages were higher—seemed like the land of opportunity.

CHANGES AND CHALLENGES

Most of these early immigrants moved to California, where their agricultural experience helped them find work in orchards and vineyards. Some of these early immigrants moved from place to place as migrant workers, following harvests and working for about eighteen cents an hour. Others even became farm managers. Sikh and small Muslim communities grew around the cities of Sacramento and Fresno. Some went to work for the lumber mills or the railroad, both of which paid better than farming. But most preferred agricultural work.

A Sikh man harvests celery in California in 1922.

THE FIVE KS

Male Sikhs traditionally follow five important practices. They are:

- Kesh—keeping the hair and beard clean and uncut
- Kangha—carrying a comb for the hair
- Kacha—wearing a shortslike undergarment
- Kara—wearing a steel bracelet symbolizing one's connection to God
- Kirpan—wearing a sword at the belt to represent righteousness

When Sikhs immigrated to America, most only continued to practice Kesh and Kara.

While these immigrants' farming skills were appreciated, Americans did not understand their cultures. The Sikhs dressed differently than most Americans, and they practiced a foreign religion. They wore turbans, and the men kept their hair long. All of these traits made it hard for Sikhs to blend into their new culture.

Muslims also found it difficult to fit into American society. Americans were predominantly Christian, and many did not understand Islam. Often they focused on one particular aspect of the religion—polygamy— to discriminate against the group. Polygamy means that a person has more than one spouse. The Quran states that a Muslim man can marry as many as four women. Although few Punjabi Muslims practiced this custom, some Americans saw all Muslims as polygamists.

These religious and cultural differences isolated Sikhs and Punjabi Muslims from mainstream America. Some people called Sikhs offensive names such as "rag heads" because of their turbans, and all immigrants from the subcontinent were often lumped together under the term "Hindoos," an inaccurate label that Muslims found especially offensive. Both Sikhs and Muslims were often forbidden to enter stores or to rent rooms. And because immigrants were usually willing to accept very low wages, many American workers were afraid of losing their own jobs. They were resentful and distrustful toward immigrants. Sometimes Sikhs and Muslims were even beaten.

Earning citizenship was another obstacle. A national law stated that only Caucasians (white people) could become citizens of the United States. Some Indian immigrants believed that this law should not apply to them, as they had been part of the British Empire. A small number of Punjabi immigrants were granted citizenship, but many more were denied. Then, when some Sikhs and Muslims who had earned enough money sent for their wives and children, they learned that the United States had passed a law ending all Asian immigration. At this news, many gave up and returned to their homeland. While others stayed, it was clear that the first flood of immigration from the Indian subcontinent to America had slowed to a trickle.

INDIAN INDEPENDENCE

Meanwhile, the struggle for independence from Britain was intensifying. In 1906 Muslim leaders created the All-India Muslim League. While the league hoped to advance Muslim political interests, it also made efforts to work with the Indian National Congress. Jinnah served as ambassador for Hindu-Muslim cooperation. Indian unity suddenly seemed more possible than ever before.

Mohammed Ali Jinnah (above) *is often called the founder of Pakistan, since he led Muslim demands for a separate state.*

But as Indian leaders began making progress, an outbreak of the deadly disease bubonic plague swept across the subcontinent. Also called the Black Death, the sickness killed hundreds of thousands of people and forced thousands of others to travel to foreign countries looking for work.

World War I (1914–1918) broke out, further hampering the league's activity. Britain declared war against Germany and its allies. As part of the British Empire, India was expected to join in the fight. More than one million men from the subcontinent—both Muslims and Hindus—fought for the British cause, having been promised a greater say in India's government after the war.

The conflict proved particularly difficult for Muslims. Britain had also declared war against the Ottoman Empire, centered in modern-day Turkey. But the Ottoman Empire was the heart of the Islamic world at the time. To many Indian Muslims, Britain's attack on the Ottomans was an attack against Islam. Anti-British feelings grew ever stronger, and more Muslims began demanding an independent Muslim state.

After World War I ended, Britain broke its promise for Indian self-government. British leaders passed new laws further limiting the population's rights. Unrest grew, and Hindus and Muslims rioted against the government. In response, the British government established martial law (rule by the military). But as new violence erupted between British soldiers and the local population, tensions neared the breaking point.

Then the unthinkable happened. In the Punjab town of Amritsar on April 13, 1919, an unarmed crowd of men, women, and children gathered for an anti–British protest. A British general, wanting to make an example of the protesters, ordered his men to open fire on the crowd. The soldiers did not stop firing until all the ammunition was used. The people—assembled in a walled park known as Jallianwala Bagh—were unable to escape. About fifteen hundred people, mostly Sikhs, were killed or wounded.

The painting below depicts the 1919 massacre, known as the Amritsar Massacre, at Jallianwala Bagh.

This violent act so outraged people across the subcontinent that it finally united all of India's factions against the British. Some people said that the British Empire died at Jallianwala Bagh.

POVERTY AND VIOLENCE

Although political unity was once again a real possibility, living conditions on the subcontinent continued to deteriorate in the 1920s. People worked long days for little money. Children as young as five were working twelve-hour days in factories and fields. While British officials lived in large houses with modern conveniences, local families of five or more people crowded together in one-room tenements (poor-quality apartments). It was not

The cramped balconies of tenements, many draped with laundry, overlook a crowded street in India.

uncommon for ten or more tenements to share one water tap. About 10 percent of the urban residents were so poor that they could not even afford these dismal lodgings. They slept on the street night after night.

More than ever, people wanted to be free of British reign, and Britain itself had come to realize that independence for India was inevitable. But Hindu and Islamic leaders still could not agree on the terms of that independence. Muslims feared that they would be powerless under a Hindu majority, just as they had been under the British. They believed a Muslim nation was the only way to ensure social, economic, and political equality for Muslims.

In 1930 the Muslim poet and philosopher Muhammad Iqbal outlined a proposal for the boundaries of an independent Muslim state. These borders were almost identical to those that would later become modern-day Pakistan.

The independence movement stalled again, however, at the onset of World War II (1939–1945). This time, the Indian National Congress refused to help Britain in the war.

NAMING A NATION

The name "Pakistan" did not exist until 1933, when law student Choudhary Rahmat Ali introduced the name in a political pamphlet for Muslim independence. The name came from the areas in and around the proposed nation. For example, *P* stood for Punjab, *A* for Afghania, and *K* for Kashmir. *Pak* also means "pure" or "holy," and the ending *-stan* means "land of," so Pakistan is often translated as "land of the pure."

But the British used the Hindu–Muslim rivalry to gain Muslim backing, and Muslim leaders agreed to aid British troops in the hope of greater support for the Muslim community after the war. To reinforce this plan, the Muslim League passed a declaration of independence in 1940. It stated that, after independence, a separate Muslim government should be established in areas with a Muslim majority.

THE BIRTH OF PAKISTAN

When World War II ended in 1945, the question of independence for India—and for Muslims—was still unresolved. As uncertainty about the future grew, Muslims and Hindus turned on each other, and riots and bloodshed between the groups were common.

At this time, Mohandas Gandhi, a Hindu leader in the independence movement, issued a new call for unity between the Hindu and Islamic communities. Gandhi urged the two groups to work together peacefully for their common goal and he opposed any plan that divided India

Independence leader Mohandas Gandhi (center front) *urged people to solve their differences without violence.*

into two separate countries. But Jinnah believed that forming two states was the only way to ensure Muslim independence. In 1946 he called for direct action to protest against the Indian congress and the British. This led to three days of riots and horrible violence between Hindus and Muslims. Thousands of people died, and British administrators decided that a Hindu–Muslim compromise would never be reached. Creating two independent nations was the only solution.

In 1947 the British declared a plan to establish two new, independent nations on the subcontinent. India would have a Hindu majority, and Pakistan would have a Muslim majority. Partition (the division between the Hindu and Muslim territories) had begun.

At the time of partition, Pakistan was divided into West Pakistan (which later became the modern-day country of Pakistan) and East Pakistan (modern-day Bangladesh). East and West Pakistan were separated by more than one thousand miles of Indian territory. An estimated 7.5 million Muslim immigrants (known

Pakistan's borders are still disputed in the twenty-first century. Download this and other maps at www. inamericabooks.com.

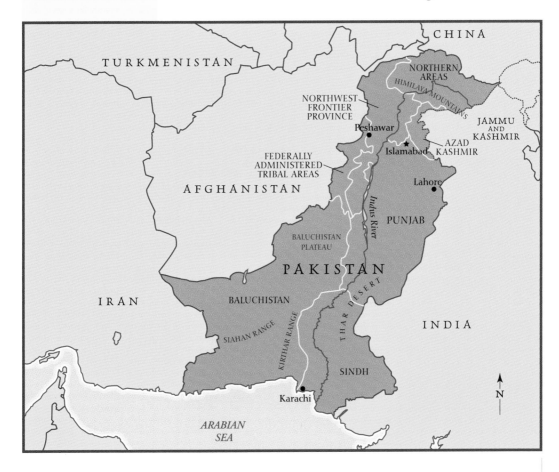

Thousands of Indian Muslims board trains for Pakistan in August 1947. Learn more about partition through links at www.inamericabooks.com.

as *muhajirs*) fled to the two parts of Pakistan, while about 10 million Hindus left these areas for India.

But the boundaries of these countries were not yet firm. Regions with a Muslim majority wanted to join Pakistan, and regions that had a Hindu majority wanted to remain part of India. But there were still several states ruled by Indian princes who answered to British administrators. These states could join either India or Pakistan, depending on the ruler's and the people's wishes.

These unclear borders led to confusion and to brutal violence in some areas. For example, the Gujarat region's Muslim prince wanted to join Pakistan. His subjects, however, were mostly Hindus and opted to become part of India. Rioting eventually led to the prince's exile to

IN OUR TOWN . . . THERE WERE STORIES OF VIOLENCE, RIOTS, ATTACKS ON TRAINS, AND BLOODSTAINED TRAINS ARRIVING WITH DEAD BODIES.

—*Saeed Suhrawardy, recalling the violence of partition*

Pakistan, and his realm was included in India. Violence also occurred as people left their homes and journeyed to their new countries. Muslims massacred trains full of Hindus leaving Pakistan, and Hindus attacked Muslims moving from India.

An atmosphere of violence and mistrust continued even after partition was complete. Some people began to wonder if life might be better outside of the subcontinent altogether. To many, America once again seemed like a land of opportunity.

For Punjabi Muslims already living in America, partition was a difficult time. They feared for their loved ones living on the subcontinent. And their homeland would never again be the same—particularly since the boundary cut across their home province. But they were also proud of their new, independent nation.

LEAVING PAKISTAN

Immediately after partition, only a small number of Pakistani Muslims immigrated to America. One reason was that, as a new nation, Pakistan needed its well-educated people to help run the new country. Skilled laborers, doctors, teachers, and scholars were essential in creating the country's economic and political base. And most Muslims were happy to finally have their own nation.

In addition, leaving East and West Pakistan for America was very expensive. Few Pakistanis could

The creation of the new state has placed a tremendous responsibility on the citizens of Pakistan. It gives them an opportunity to demonstrate to the world how a nation containing many elements can live in peace . . . irrespective of caste or creed.

—Mohammed Ali Jinnah, who became Pakistan's first governor-general, in a speech in August 1947

afford the trip. And as a people with a cultural history thousands of years old, they had many social guidelines governing marriage, occupation, diet, and methods of worship that would be difficult to follow in a foreign land. To make the trip to the United States, a person had to be courageous and flexible—as well as somewhat financially independent.

Often the decision for one person to emigrate (to leave one's country and settle elsewhere) was made by an entire family. Extended family was a very important social structure for Pakistanis. Children were considered an investment in the group's future, and individuals sometimes set aside their own wishes for the good of the whole family. When one family member emigrated, relatives often pooled their resources to fund the journey. In return, Pakistani immigrants in America sent money back home to help family members who still lived there.

Even for Pakistanis with enough money, emigration could be difficult. Getting the right permits for travel to the United States was often hard. At the time, some Americans were unhappy with the large number of immigrants arriving from Asia— including the subcontinent. Some of these Americans were still worried about newcomers taking jobs away from them. Others did not like the way the country's ethnic makeup was changing. As a result, the U.S. government had passed several laws restricting the number of non-European immigrants who could enter the country.

The Pakistani government presented another obstacle. The government encouraged students to travel abroad for study but discouraged permanent emigration. Politicians and social leaders feared that the developing country would lose its best and brightest to foreign countries. The loss of these highly educated and skilled people, particularly doctors, engineers, and scientists, would seriously damage the growing economy and social system.

For these reasons, only about twenty-five hundred Pakistanis moved to the United States between 1947 and 1965. Many of these people settled near each other, and new Pakistani communities formed in New York City, Chicago, and parts of California. Large urban areas appealed to this group of immigrants because big cities usually offered more jobs than smaller towns did. Better public transportation was also usually available in these areas. Many Pakistani immigrants found inexpensive housing in the cities' apartment buildings and row houses (narrow side-by-side dwellings that often share walls).

In the 1950s, many Pakistani immigrants to America were students. The United States offered more opportunities for freedom and higher learning than Pakistan did. Most of these young people planned to earn degrees and return to Pakistan. But once they graduated, many were offered well-paying jobs in America. Some had grown attached to their new home in the United States, where they had made friends and other connections. Many of these people decided to stay.

MANY PEOPLE ARE INTERESTED IN LEARNING ABOUT THEIR FAMILY'S HISTORY. THIS STUDY IS CALLED GENEALOGY. IF YOU'D LIKE TO LEARN ABOUT YOUR OWN GENEALOGY AND HOW YOUR ANCESTORS CAME TO AMERICA, VISIT WWW.INAMERICABOOKS.COM FOR TIPS AND LINKS TO HELP YOU GET STARTED.

ACCIDENTAL IMMIGRANTS

In 1958 senior military officials took over Pakistan's government, launching a decade of political instability and military rule. Many scholars and professionals left the country during this time, fearing a government backlash against their more liberal ideas. Many chose to move—temporarily—to America until Pakistan's political situation settled down. But once in the United States, many appreciated a newfound freedom of expression, which they had not had under Pakistan's military leaders. They became accustomed to the greater rights that their new country offered. Those who had believed that America was a temporary stop often decided to stay.

Others did return to their homeland, only to find that the economic opportunities they had in America did not exist in Pakistan. Engineers and doctors discovered that their advanced degrees did not guarantee them better-paying jobs in their homeland as they did in the United States. Disappointed, some of these Pakistanis went back to America.

LIFE IN AMERICA

While America offered many opportunities, life there was rarely easy for new immigrants. Many Americans at this time were prejudiced against minorities, including people of African, Asian, and Native American heritage. Because Pakistani immigrants wore different clothing and had darker skin than many other Americans, they were often discriminated against in housing, in hotels, and in restaurants. Some Americans believed that these immigrants should not be part of American society at all.

Religious differences probably presented the biggest challenge for these immigrants. Pakistani Americans were usually devout Muslims. Islam dictated how they prayed, dressed, ate, and conducted themselves—sometimes at the expense of "fitting in" to their new, usually Christian-dominated communities. Most Americans were suspicious of or uneducated about Islam. Some still considered Pakistani men polygamists.

In addition, Pakistanis and other Americans did not tend to interact very much socially. American society felt too open to many Pakistanis, sometimes going against their religious or cultural customs. Instead, most Pakistani immigrants chose to socialize primarily with their families and with other Pakistani Americans.

Most members of this early immigrant group settled in New York City, specifically along Coney Island Avenue in Brooklyn. Families of four often settled into small, one-bedroom apartments or in basement apartments to save on rent. More financially comfortable families rented small private houses.

Some Pakistani Americans choose to socialize mainly with other Pakistani Americans.

In this area, small grocery stores and gift shops quickly sprang up to sell spices and goods familiar to Pakistani immigrants. Restaurants catering to Pakistani Americans opened for business. Community members started a mosque (an Islamic place of worship) in a basement. The empty storefronts and row houses that had once filled this run-down neighborhood were soon bustling with activity.

Brooklyn's Coney Island Avenue boasts many Pakistani grocery stores and other shops.

As they settled into their new home, Pakistani Americans did modify some of their old traditions. One change was the Pakistani American attitude toward women. In Pakistan, men and women are often separated from each other, according to Islamic law as well as some Hindu traditions. Unrelated men and women rarely, if ever, mingled. Some families practiced purdah, a custom that required women to stay within their homes and limited social interaction to their family unit as much as possible. Many women wore veils over their faces in the presence of male family members other than their husbands.

To go outside, Pakistani women from strict families were required to wear a burka, a heavy head-to-toe cover with small slits near the eyes for vision. For others, wearing the *salwar kameez*, a combination of loose trousers and a long tunic, was acceptable, though women were expected to cover their heads with a scarf called a *dupatta* when they went outside. These clothes fit traditional Pakistani ideas about modesty for women.

In America, however, Pakistani women began to enjoy more freedom. To help support their families, many women took jobs outside the home—making it almost impossible to avoid contact with men outside their families. And Pakistani American women were allowed to attend religious services with men, a practice unheard of in Pakistan.

Yet, while Pakistani women in America had increased freedom, many traditions were still practiced. Women generally did not leave the house when their husbands were not home. Working, shopping, doctor visits, taking children to school, and similar activities were considered necessary and therefore accepted. But visiting friends, going to see a movie, or other leisure activities were not considered proper trips for a Pakistani American woman to make alone.

Pakistani American women also faced other unique challenges. For many, isolation and loneliness were problems. Women living in Pakistan were seldom alone. Extended families often lived together or near each other, and grandmothers, aunts, and female cousins were an important part of a woman's social network. In America things were different. Families were separated by an ocean, and women often lost their traditional support systems and companionship. They found themselves almost completely alone—neither part of their traditional society nor part of their new home. In addition, many women chose to continue wearing Pakistani dress, including the salwar kameez and especially the dupatta. And because many traditional families believed that a girl's place was in the home and not in the classroom, few Pakistani women who moved to America spoke fluent English. All of these

After tomorrow, thousands of miles of ocean would separate her from everything and everyone she had ever known. . . . Sadika's idea about America came from romance novels, television programs and snatches of overheard conversation, and she did not see how she could find a niche for herself. . . .

—*from* Sadika's Way: A Novel of Pakistan and America *by Hina Haq*

factors made it difficult for Pakistani women to feel like a part of American culture.

Pakistani men, on the other hand, often exchanged their traditional garb for American-style clothing. Many professionals wore business suits and ties for work. Jeans or casual dress pants became standard for leisure time. Men also abandoned their customary sandals for dress shoes or tennis shoes.

All of these adjustments to the culture of their new homeland was a major challenge for Pakistani Americans. But the first waves of Pakistani immigrants did have some advantages over arrivals from other countries. Learning a new language, for example, was not as big an obstacle for them as it was for many other immigrant groups. As former British territories, India and Pakistan had used English in business and government, both before and after partition. As a result, many male Pakistanis already spoke fluent English when they arrived in America. This knowledge helped them join the mainstream workforce

This family is a good example of the differences sometimes found between Pakistani men and women in the United States. The man wears American-style clothing, while the women are dressed in the traditional salwar kameez.

TO DISCOVER SOME OF THE MANY STORIES OF PAKISTANIS MIGRATING TO THE UNITED STATES, VISIT WWW.INAMERICABOOKS.COM FOR LINKS.

more quickly and find better-paying jobs than immigrants who did not know English.

Another advantage for this first major wave was that many of these Pakistani immigrants were well-educated professionals who had come from Pakistan's big cities, such as Karachi and Lahore. In many cases, their education had exposed them to Western culture, making them somewhat more familiar with American ideas and beliefs. While Pakistani Americans faced many challenges, they were eager to build better lives for themselves and their families in their new home.

3 PAKISTANI AMERICANS

As Pakistani immigrants adjusted to their new homes in America, they developed a unique culture by blending Pakistani heritage with American customs. But one thing that did not change was the central role of the family.

Pakistani American family structures have often followed very traditional patterns, especially among early waves of immigrants. Families were usually patriarchal, with the husband and father as head of the household. And while some Pakistani American women worked outside the home, other families followed a more customary division of labor. In this system, husbands worked as providers, while women stayed at home and cared for the family and household.

Pakistani American children were expected to always be respectful to their parents and other adult relatives. They were also encouraged to develop a strong sense of family and

Many Pakistani American children have a strong sense of their heritage. These young girls watch a New York City parade celebrating the anniversary of Pakistan's independence.

community. Most learned the language of their parents, as well as English. Mosques taught them to read Arabic—the language of the Quran—and they usually accompanied their parents to Islamic events, Pakistani holidays, and other celebrations.

To help keep family ties strong, Pakistani Americans often made a point of eating the main meal of the day together. This habit gave family members the chance to visit, share news, and enjoy traditional Pakistani food. Preparing authentic Pakistani meals still required a good deal of time and labor. Some cooks adopted American conveniences such as canned foods, but certain ingredients, such as special spices and rice, could only be found at stores that catered to the Pakistani American community.

Pakistani families gather for a picnic. Family and community are both very important aspects of Pakistani American culture.

Leisure activities for Pakistani American families often involved visiting other relatives or attending community events. Extended family, including grandparents, aunts, uncles, and cousins, was almost as important as immediate family. When members of an extended family lived apart from each other, phone calls and letters kept them connected. Visits were also encouraged. Siblings and close relatives living in Pakistan traveled to America as often as possible, sometimes staying for long periods of time. In turn, many Pakistani Americans—particularly first-generation immigrants—took weeks off from work to return to Pakistan. All of these things helped Pakistani Americans maintain close ties to their homeland and heritage.

Maintaining a strong cultural heritage led to a strong community. Over the decades, Pakistani Americans opened many small businesses, such as restaurants, grocery stores, and gift shops, to serve the immigrant community. Mosques and Islamic centers were built. In New York City, Brooklyn's Midwood neighborhood along Coney Island Avenue became home to so many Pakistani Americans that it was nicknamed Little Pakistan.

Filled with the sights and sounds of home, Little Pakistan became a haven for New York's Pakistani Americans. Aromas of familiar spices such as saffron and rosewater filled the air. Friday afternoon worshippers filled the mosque on Coney Island Avenue to overflowing, forcing latecomers to spill out onto the sidewalk with their prayer rugs.

Many Pakistani American Muslims practice the second pillar of Islam, or praying toward Mecca five times per day.

Families gathered after services to enjoy a late-afternoon snack, filling the many restaurants along the avenue. All of this helped Pakistani Americans feel more at home in their new land.

THE BIG WAVE

In the mid–1900s, the Pakistani American community still remained relatively small. But change was on the way. In the 1960s, minority groups in America began demanding equal rights. This period, known as the civil rights movement, led to many changes in the laws of the land—including those regarding immigration. A new immigration law in 1965 especially affected Pakistanis. It ended the old national quotas, which had severely limited the number of immigrants coming from non–European countries. It also made it easier for relatives of immigrants who had become U.S. citizens to join their families in America, as well as allowing entrance for more numbers of refugees (people fleeing from political, economic, racial, or religious persecution). Following the law's introduction, the number of South Asian immigrants skyrocketed. Among these new arrivals were thousands of Pakistanis. In fact, the largest wave of Pakistani immigration began in 1965.

The Pakistani government also began changing its attitude toward emigration around this time. By the 1970s, the government realized that the money nonresidents were sending back to their families was an important source of funds for the nation. As a result, the government decided to loosen restrictions on emigration and it allowed nonresident Pakistanis to maintain dual nationality. In other words, emigrants could be citizens of both Pakistan and the United States (or other any country where they had moved).

The majority of Pakistani immigrants who arrived in the United States with this wave were highly educated. Many had degrees in fields such as engineering, science, and medicine. These new immigrants settled mainly in large urban areas, especially those that already had Pakistani American communities. New York City, Chicago, Los Angeles, and San Francisco all remained home to large populations of Pakistani immigrants. Living near other Pakistani families gave new arrivals a built-in support system, as well as provided nearby Pakistani stores, restaurants, and community organizations.

By 1970 about twenty thousand Pakistanis were living in

Many Pakistani immigrants work in fields that require advanced education. This Pakistani-born doctor works at a clinic in New Hampshire.

America. The new laws had allowed many Pakistani American citizens to bring their parents or other family members over. But events back in Pakistan also played a huge part in immigration. In the Punjab region—where nearly half of all Pakistani Americans came from—drought and famine had once again forced people to seek better

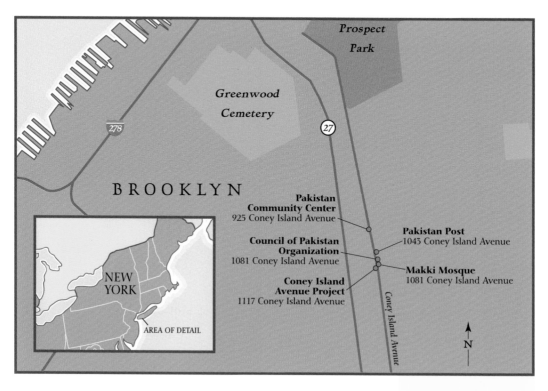

Brooklyn, New York, is home to many Pakistani Americans. The map above shows the locations of a few key Pakistani American organizations. Visit www.inamericabooks.com to download this and other maps.

opportunities abroad. Then, in the early 1970s, devastating political strife broke out in Pakistan.

Since partition, a political and cultural rift had gradually been widening between East and West Pakistan. Aside from religion, the two parts of Pakistan had little connection to each other. West Pakistan had gained control of the country's central government, armed forces, and economy, while the more densely populated East Pakistan was much poorer and held little power. Resentful of West Pakistan's control over them, East Pakistanis, known

I HAD MY SUITCASE IN MY HAND, $50 IN MY POCKET, AND I KNEW NO ONE.

—*Hassan Zee, a Pakistani American filmmaker, describing his arrival in the United States* as Bengalis, began to push for independence.

In March 1971, civil war erupted between East and West Pakistan. Thousands of people were killed as Bengali liberation forces fought West Pakistan's troops. The nine-month conflict finally won independence for East Pakistan, which became known as Bangladesh, while West Pakistan became simply Pakistan. But the violence left both nations deeply scarred. About one million Bengalis were killed. Another ten million fled to India. And people from both Bangladesh and Pakistan fled to the United States. America once again saw an influx of Pakistani immigrants.

Members of this second wave tended to be less educated and less fluent in English than earlier Pakistani immigrants. This disadvantage limited their employment opportunities. Many took jobs as semiskilled or unskilled workers in restaurants, shops, gas stations, and dry cleaners. In California many worked in the state's fruit orchards and vegetable fields, just as earlier Punjabi immigrants had.

BORDERLINE

India and Pakistan disagree over their shared border in the state of Jammu and Kashmir. A treaty in 1972 divided the land between the two countries. But both India and Pakistan disagree about the division, and fighting between these two neighbors remains a problem for the region. This violence and political tension between these countries, which has continued into the twenty-first century, was yet another factor in Pakistani emigration to America.

A Growing Community

Even after the major wave of immigration in the 1960s and 1970s began to slow, Pakistanis continued to come to America. According to the 1990 U.S. census, about 100,000 Pakistani Americans lived in the United States. The true number was probably much higher, however, and as many as 500,000 to 750,000 Pakistanis may have actually lived in the United States at that time.

Many Pakistani American families live comfortable lives. For most, owning a house is an important symbol of success. Families tend to take care of each other, often going into business together. Many Pakistani American students graduate from college, and most do not have student loans to pay back. Community members usually prefer to turn to fellow Pakistani Americans for financial help rather than government agencies.

Pakistani Americans may own their own businesses or work in scientific fields, particularly medicine and engineering. Pakistani Americans have also founded and

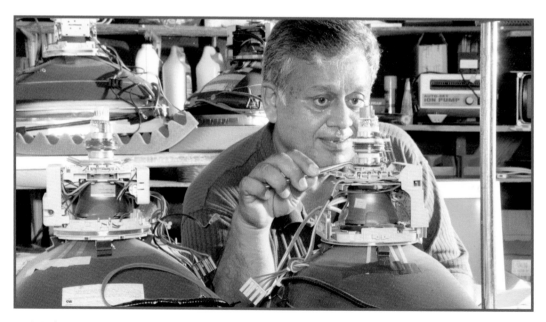

A Pakistani American electrical engineer wires television sets in his small shop in Laguna Hills, California.

run very successful businesses. For example, NexGen—
—a leader in computer–chip manufacturing—was
started by a Pakistani American.

As their numbers continued to increase,
Pakistani Americans also began to gain greater
political influence. In the early years of Pakistani
immigration, the community had been too small to
have much impact on U.S. politics. However, many
Pakistanis had taken part in the political scene,
joining struggles for civil rights and involving
themselves in local politics. As time went on, their
role grew. In 1994 two Pakistani Americans were
appointed to state positions in Illinois. The
community has also funded candidates for office in
areas with large Pakistani American populations,
particularly in Brooklyn, New York.

Pakistani Muslims have played an important role
in the development of Islamic political groups in
America and in the leadership of mosques. They have
founded important Islamic centers and have
participated in interfaith dialogues in the hope of
explaining their faith and culture to their fellow
Americans. Pakistani Americans have headed some of
the leading Muslim organizations, such as the Islamic
Society of North America, the American Muslim
Alliance, and the United Muslims of America. They
have helped their own communities better
understand and appreciate the differences of other
religious groups. All of these efforts have helped Islam
adapt and grow within American society.

Cultural, educational, and professional organizations are also strengthening the community. Most major universities have a Pakistani Students Association. Large cities often have Pakistani American Associations, while the Pakistani American Congress is a national organization. More than twenty newspapers and other publications also help unite the community, the largest of which is the English–Urdu publication *Pakistan Link*. Online newspapers such as *Dawn* also serve as links between America and Pakistan. All of these organizations help support Pakistani Americans through encouraging a greater understanding of cultural, religious, and ethnic differences.

FIND LINKS TO THE LATEST PAKISTANI NEWS AT WWW.INAMERICABOOKS.COM.

Many community organizations serve both the Pakistani American community and the immigrants' homeland. For example, in the early and mid–1990s, Pakistani Americans helped create temporary governments in Pakistan when the political climate of the country was unstable. Other Pakistani American groups have helped establish health and education programs in Pakistan to maintain a strong connection to their homeland.

ISLAM IN AMERICA

Most Pakistani Americans are Muslims, and their faith has been a unifying force in many ways. The Quran requires Muslims to pray five times every day, while facing in the direction of Mecca, Saudi Arabia—Islam's holiest city. In addition, many Muslims visit the mosque at least once a week, usually on Friday afternoons.

FRUIT *CHAAT*

This sweet and spicy fruit salad is popular among Pakistani Americans. Any fresh fruit in season can be used for this tasty dish. To learn how to prepare other Pakistani dishes, visit www.inamericabooks.com for links.

1 BANANA

1 APPLE

1 PEAR

1 PEACH

1 ORANGE

1 CUP GRAPES

3 TO 4 TABLESPOONS SUGAR

1 TEASPOON GROUND CUMIN

PINCH OF SALT

$1/4$ TEASPOON BLACK PEPPER

A FEW DROPS OF LEMON JUICE OR

ORANGE JUICE

1. Cut the fruit into bite-sized pieces and put in a medium-sized bowl.
2. In a smaller bowl, mix the sugar, cumin, salt, pepper, and juice together. Add this mixture to the fruit and stir well.

Serves 3 to 4

In communities that do not have mosques, Pakistani American Muslims make a point of visiting the nearest mosque on important religious holidays.

But often these mosques serve a larger Muslim community than Pakistani Americans alone. Pakistani Muslims pray alongside Arab American Muslims, African American Muslims, and other groups of Muslims. This interaction with other Islamic groups can occasionally present challenges. Pakistanis have sometimes had to confront long-standing tensions with Muslims of different ethnicity or from different sects of Islam. For example, most Pakistanis belong to the Sunni sect, but they often share worship space with Shiite Muslims. To overcome these differences, some Pakistani Americans choose to focus on Islam's shared fundamental beliefs rather than the much more specific rituals and rules of a particular sect. Younger Pakistani Americans, in particular, tend to be tolerant of other Muslim sects and other religions.

Important events in the Pakistani American community are usually based on Islam. Weddings and funerals follow traditional Muslim rituals. For example, when a community member dies, only men participate in the burial ceremony. Often, especially for those immigrants who maintained close ties to their homeland, the body might be flown to Pakistan for burial.

In addition, Islamic holidays in the Pakistani American community are held in much the same way as they are in Pakistan. The most important of these events is Ramadan, the holiest month in the Islamic year. During Ramadan, most Muslims fast, meaning that they do not eat or drink between sunrise and sunset. The month is a time of prayer and worship. Another important holiday is Eid al-Fitr, a festival celebrating the end of Ramadan.

TO DISCOVER MORE ABOUT PAKISTANI CULTURAL TRADITIONS IN AMERICA, VISIT WWW.INAMERICABOOKS.COM FOR LINKS.

Many Pakistani Americans decorate their hands and feet with mehndi for special occasions, such as weddings and holidays.

Children receive gifts, and girls and women may decorate their hands with patterns called *mehndi*, painted with a reddish dye called henna. Families eat a special meal together, and food and money is given to the poor.

CAUGHT BETWEEN CULTURES

Living in the United States is a balancing act for most Pakistani Americans. Second-generation Pakistani Americans (children born to immigrant parents) are still trying to carve out their own cultural identity. America is their home, but Pakistan is their heritage. Mixing the two often proves to be a difficult task.

One of the biggest obstacles for Pakistani Americans is their attitude about American society. While most Pakistani Americans admire and appreciate aspects of American life, such as political and social freedom, they may be uneasy about other aspects of their new home. Many Muslim parents see some American customs and values as deeply opposed to their own beliefs and even potentially dangerous to their way of life. For example, Pakistani Americans expect their children to be respectful and modest. To them American children may seem too outspoken, disrespectful, or independent. To encourage their children to follow more traditional ways, many Pakistani American parents teach them about their history and heritage at an early age. In some communities, weekend classes educate Pakistani American children about their Pakistani identity, often by teaching Islam and Urdu. Despite this, some Muslim students in mainstream American schools hide their religious beliefs to blend in better. Children may also want to be called by different, more "American" sounding names to hide their ethnicity.

YOU CAN FIND TIPS ON RESEARCHING NAMES IN YOUR FAMILY HISTORY AT WWW.INAMERICABOOKS.COM.

Another concern for Pakistani American parents is the openness of American society, especially regarding dating. At the time that girls would traditionally be separated from boys and taken out of school in Pakistan, many American teens begin to date. Because American law requires that all students attend school until they are at least sixteen years old, interaction between boys and girls is unavoidable unless private schools are available—and affordable. When private school is not an option, parents sometimes pull their daughters out of school in about the seventh grade and educate them at home. For some girls, the shift can mean the end of their education entirely.

Dating and marrying outside the Pakistani American community—and outside the family's religious and ethnic subgroups—is usually frowned upon. Parents often consult relatives and friends about prospective spouses for their children, and many families prefer arranged marriages. American Muslims organize special summer camps, social gatherings, and marriage advertisements to help young Muslims find partners. But even these Muslim institutions have a difficult time keeping boys and girls apart. The divorce rate for this group remains very low compared to the general U.S. population. But some American-born children of Pakistani immigrants would rather not have their parents involved. They may seek the freedom to date whomever they choose.

Ethnic tension and stereotyping among different Pakistani subgroups have also proved a problem for Pakistani Americans. Although the Pakistani American community often works together for certain causes, many Pakistani immigrants spend

the majority of their personal time with members of their own regional or ethnic groups. In other words, most Sindhis prefer to spend their time with other Sindhis, and Punjabis tend to stick with other Punjabis. Within the larger Pakistani American community, Sindhis and Baluchis are considered more conservative, while those from cities

I have to admit that we socialize almost entirely with other Pakistanis. . . . And when we do, the rules from Pakistan still apply. You can see the cultural differences between people from different regions. . . . Since so many of us go back and forth, we are still very much shaped by Pakistan.

—Hassan, a Pakistani American immigrant

in the Punjab might be seen as more liberal. In addition, Pakistani immigrants from rural areas often view those from Pakistan's cities as too open and westernized. These preconceived ideas can often cause tension.

A similar tension happens between first-generation immigrants and their children. For example, most first-generation Pakistani Americans believe it is important to travel back to their native land as often as financially possible. They bring gifts to family and friends and contribute to Pakistani organizations and charities. They take a deep interest in the politics and society of Pakistan.

But second-generation immigrants do not have this same strong connection to Pakistan. They consider America home. They travel to Pakistan less frequently than their parents and they tend to distance themselves from the nation's politics. Ethnic tensions—especially among Pakistani subgroups and between Pakistanis and Indians—have lessened among the children of Pakistani immigrants, who tend to be more open to accepting people from different ethnic backgrounds. And younger Pakistani Americans are often drawn to more aspects of American culture, bringing them into conflict with their more traditional older relatives. Finding a middle ground between America and Pakistan is an ongoing challenge for all Pakistani Americans.

A New Type of Discrimination

On September 11, 2001, terrorists crashed airplanes into the World Trade Center in New York City and the

Pentagon near Washington, D.C. These acts of violence killed thousands of people and shocked the world. They also suddenly brought several of America's ethnic groups—including Pakistani Americans—into the spotlight.

After the terrorist attacks, the Pakistani American community faced greater discrimination than ever before. Because the terrorists had been Muslims and because Pakistan had supported other terrorist groups, the American public became fearful and suspicious of Pakistani immigrants. Thousands of Pakistani Americans left the United States after the attacks, fearing retaliation, unfair arrests, and even violence.

The U.S. government soon did change some rules that affected Pakistanis. In the months following the attacks, the government announced that immigrants from certain Muslim countries—including Pakistan—had to register with the Immigration and Naturalization Service (INS). (The INS is now known as U.S.

Immigrants from many different countries wait to register with the INS outside its offices in New York City. Many Pakistani Americans had to register after the September 11 attacks.

Citizenship and Immigration Services.) The goal of the policy was to strengthen homeland security by keeping a closer eye on immigrant communities. To register, immigrants visited their local INS office, where they had to answer specific questions about where they live and where they pray. Male immigrants who were over the age of sixteen and who had arrived before October 2001 had to go through a special registration process. And if immigrants wanted to apply for visas (documents allowing immigrants to stay in the country for a limited time), they had to answer more in-depth questions.

As a result of this change, many Pakistanis who were in the country on a temporary basis were deported (returned) to Pakistan—often with little or no warning. Some had stayed longer than their visas allowed them to or had other paperwork problems.

In addition, the government started singling out Muslim men between the ages of eighteen and thirty-three, believing they were the group most likely to have links to terrorist organizations. Parents of young Muslim men feared losing their sons, as more than one thousand men were detained (held for questioning), often for weeks. Many of them were Pakistani. Some of those who did find themselves detained spent their life's savings on lawyers to help them avoid being deported. Yet even after paying more than ten thousand dollars each, most detainees were still deported.

The government passed the USA Patriot Act in 2001. This new law allowed government agents more freedom to investigate suspected terrorists. For example, investigators could tap phone and computer lines and could more easily obtain business records. The act also increased penalties for those who commit and aid crimes of terrorism. In Pakistani American communities, the fear of being watched or detained made an already tense environment even more uncomfortable.

New laws were not the only problems Pakistani Americans dealt with after the September 11 attacks. Especially in the first months, increased racial prejudice made daily life difficult for Pakistani immigrants. Some Pakistani American boys no longer wanted to use Muhammad (a common Pakistani name) at school. Many became targets for teasing and bullying. Some Pakistani businesses struggled as their Pakistani clients returned to Pakistan or as other American customers began staying away. And more Pakistani American men were rounded up and detained for questioning by government agencies, such as the Federal Bureau of Investigation (FBI). Angry comments were sometimes directed at women wearing traditional Pakistani dress in public.

Several Pakistani immigrants even lost their lives in response to the terrorist attacks. A shop owner named Waqar Hasan was shot and killed in Dallas, Texas, four days after the September 11 attacks. The gunman, Mark Anthony Stroman, said that he shot Hasan in retaliation for the terrorist attacks.

Another Pakistani, swept up in a wave of arrests targeting Muslim immigrants in Coney Island, New York, died in prison a few days after Hasan's murder. Although officials said that the man had suffered a heart attack, his family believed that he might have been mistreated.

Pakistan's government denounced the September 11 attacks and agreed to become an important partner in the U.S. war against terrorism. Yet many Pakistani

Americans find themselves unable to settle back into their lives. Organizations such as the Islamic Circle of North America have worked to strengthen the community through financial and legal support. And in 2002, Pakistan's president, General Pervez Musharraf, visited with U.S. president George W. Bush to address the problems that the Pakistani American community faced. In response, President Bush promised that the American public would not take action against the Pakistani American community. And while many Pakistani Americans declare that they will stay in their new homeland, many feel they have been unfairly singled out since September 11.

The impact of September 11 still haunts the Pakistani American community. Once home to roughly one hundred thousand Pakistanis, Little Pakistan had lost an estimated forty-five hundred people by 2005. Some were deported, while others left voluntarily—but sadly—feeling

I feel a difference since 9/11. I have to explain myself here in a way that my parents never had to, even though my parents were immigrants. . . . I thought after I accepted U.S. citizenship that was the end of it, and now I am not particularly sure.

—*Malika, a Pakistani American woman describing the aftermath of the terrorist attacks of September 11, 2001*

that tension and fear for their families left them little choice.

In Little Pakistan, attendance at Friday afternoon services has dropped significantly. The mosque is no longer overflowing. Restaurants close early, and businesses of all types have lost nearly 40 percent of their customers. Signs in the neighborhood advertise houses for rent and help wanted. Many Pakistani Americans live in uncertainty, feeling that their way of life is still closely watched by the government and even by their fellow Americans.

THE FUTURE

The Pakistani American community is relatively young, yet it is a strong and dynamic group. Its people have added immeasurably to America's intellectual wealth, as Pakistani American scientists improve our lives and expand our knowledge. Pakistani immigrants own and operate important businesses and make contributions to the information technology industry through important scholarship and inventions. They are also working to develop understanding between Islam and other religious groups through interfaith dialogues and strong community organizations.

Nevertheless, Pakistani Americans still face an uncertain future in many ways. Second- and third-generation immigrants have to find a balance between their Muslim identity and their American surroundings. In the wake of the September 11 terrorist attacks, they must struggle to gain the trust and respect of other Americans. They will need to rebuild and bolster their communities if they are to find their voice in American politics. Yet, despite these obstacles, the Pakistani American community remains proud of its past and hopeful about its future.

IT IS EASIER TO FOLLOW YOUR DREAMS IN THE UNITED STATES THAN IN ANY OTHER COUNTRY IN THE WORLD. . . . YOU CAN LIVE YOUR OWN LIFE, FOLLOW YOUR OWN TRADITIONS, AND PRAY AT ANY PLACE YOU WANT WITHOUT ANY TROUBLE.

—*Adeel Bhutta, a Pakistani American student*

FAMOUS PAKISTANI AMERICANS

MOHAMMAD AKHTER (b. 1944)

Mohammad Akhter was born in India but his family moved to Pakistan following partition. After earning his medical degree in Lahore, he moved to the United States. In the 1970s and 1980s, he served in the state health departments of Michigan and Missouri, and in 1991 he became commissioner of public health in Washington, D.C. As commissioner he created mobile medical clinics to provide health care services to poor neighborhoods. He also started a school health project providing city schools with nurses and health education, and created a citywide program to provide immunizations to children. Dr. Akhter is the executive director of the American Public Health Association and cochair of the Medicine and Public Health Initiative (MPHI). He is the president and chief executive officer (CEO) of InterAction, which provides humanitarian and development assistance in developing countries.

SABU DASTAGIR (1924–1963)

Sabu Dastagir was born in southern India, but he claimed Pakistan as his homeland after partition. At the age of twelve, Sabu was discovered by a director looking for a young boy for the lead in his movie *Elephant Boy*. The movie soon made Sabu an international star. He played Abu in his second film, *The Thief of Bagdad*, and then appeared as Mowgli in the movie version of Rudyard Kipling's *Jungle Book*. In 1944 Sabu received

American citizenship following enlistment in the U.S. Army Air Force. While in the service, he flew more than forty missions in the South Pacific and was awarded the Distinguished Flying Cross. His final role was Ram Singh in the 1964 film *A Tiger Walks*.

ZULFIKAR GHOSE (b. 1935)

Zulfikar Ghose is a Pakistani American English–language writer. Born in Sialkot to Muslim parents, he moved to Bombay, India, in 1942.

After partition, Ghose moved to the United States in 1969, where he became a professor of English at the University of Texas at Austin. He writes poetry, novels, and nonfiction, including biographies and books of literary criticism. His works include *The Loss of India, Jets from Orange: Poems, The Murder of Aziz Khan,* and *A Memory of Asia, New and Selected Poems.*

AMANULLAH KHAN (b. 1940)

Dr. Amanullah Khan is a physician and author who has received many awards and has held various leadership positions. He received medical degrees from Pakistan's King Edward Medical College and from Baylor University in Texas. After establishing a thriving medical practice in Dallas, Texas, he served as a member of the Texas Board of Health. Dr. Khan also served on the President's Advisory Commission on Asian Americans and Pacific Islanders, and was president of the Association of Pakistani Physicians of North America. His professional awards include the Presidential Gold Medal from the Pakistan Academy of Medical Sciences.

MOHAMMAD ASAD KHAN

(b. 1940) Mohammad Asad Khan is a physicist and college professor at the University of Hawaii. He has also served as a visiting scientist at the National Aeronautics and Space Administration's Goddard Space Flight Center and served on the Hawaii Environmental Council. In addition to his work in the United States, Khan has worked as the minister of petroleum and natural resources for Pakistan. In 1979 Khan was a founding member of the Muslim Students' Association of Hawaii (MSA), which became the Muslim Association of Hawaii (MAH) in 1990. The MSA, formed by a group of Muslim students from around the world, became the first official organization to represent Hawaii's Muslim population. The group was instrumental in establishing the Manoa mosque near the University of Hawaii.

HAFEEZ MALIK (b. 1931) Dr.

Hafeez Malik is an authority on the Muslim world and Islamic studies. He received a journalism degree from Pakistan's University of the Punjab and served as public relations officer for the city of Lahore. In 1953 he moved to America to go to graduate school, and from 1958 to 1961, he was the White House correspondent for two Pakistani daily newspapers. In 1961 Dr. Malik received his doctorate in political science. Since then he has served as a visiting professor in the Foreign Service Institute of the U.S. State Department and as a professor of political science at Pennsylvania's Villanova University. He speaks seven languages and has published four books and many papers in his field.

SAMINA QURAESHI (b. 1946)

Samina Quraeshi is an artist, author, and designer who holds both Pakistani and American citizenship.

In addition to owning her own graphic design consulting firm, she has served as the director of design arts at the National Endowment for the Arts in Washington, D.C., and as a design consultant to the Pakistani government. She has written papers and given speeches about the role of women in Pakistan, as well as the importance of art in community. In 1997 she received a Progressive Architecture Award, and her work on a design project working with rural communities won her a Planning Award for Public Education. Since 1999 she has served as the Henry R. Luce Professor in Family and Community at the University of Miami. One of her main goals is to help develop networks to better serve inner-city communities and families.

MOHAMMED SAYEED QURAISHI (b. 1924) Dr.

Mohammed Sayeed Quraishi is a physician who studied at the University of Massachusetts. He served as a member of the United Nations World Health Organization team in Bangladesh and has worked at the National Institutes of Health in Maryland. Dr. Quraishi has also written books and articles on science and medicine.

ATIQ RAZA (b. 1950) Atiq Raza is

one of the most famous and most successful Pakistani American businesspeople. Born in Lahore, Raza moved to America in the late 1970s to study. Since earning his master's degree from Stanford University in California, Raza has gone on to serve as president of Advanced Micro Devices, has founded NexGen, a

computer software company, and has established Raza Foundries, a firm that invests in Internet start-up companies. He is the founder, chairman, and CEO of Raza Microelectronics, Inc. He also serves on the board of directors of several other companies.

BAPSI SIDHWA (b. 1938) Known as Pakistan's leading English-language novelist, Bapsi Sidhwa has gained international acclaim for her novels *The Crow Eaters, The Bride,* and *Cracking India.* Sidhwa moved to the United States in 1983. Her first three novels take place in Pakistan and explore the dramatic events leading up to partition and the birth of Pakistan. *Cracking India* received numerous awards, was declared a New York Times Notable Book for 1991, and was adapted into a 1998 motion picture called *Earth.* Sidhwa's fourth novel, *An American Brat,* follows the experiences of an immigrant girl in the late 1970s. In addition to her novels, Sidhwa has published articles and short stories. She also received the Sitara-i-Imtiaz, Pakistan's highest national honor in the field of arts and has taught at several U.S. universities.

HASSAN ZEE (b. 1971) Hassan Zee is a writer, producer, and director, who has worked in radio, television, and film in his relatively short career. Born in Chakwal, Pakistan, Zee studied medicine. But his real passion was writing for Radio Pakistan. His work there led to an offer to do an AIDS awareness film for the Ministry of Culture. In 1996 Zee wrote, directed,  and produced the film titled *The Dim Light,* which was shown in twenty-three countries. Soon afterward, Zee moved to the United States to pursue his dream of filmmaking. He worked as a medical assistant in San Francisco while he worked on his first feature film, *Night of Henna.* Released in 2005, *Night of Henna* explores the culture clash in a Pakistani American family as a young woman's parents arrange her wedding. Zee is currently working on a film titled *Strange Feelings.*

TIMELINE

2500 B.C.	Humans begin establishing the Indus civilization in the area that would later become Pakistan.
1700 B.C.	The Indus civilization ends.
A.D. 600s	The prophet Muhammad founds Islam.
1000s–1200s	Muslim forces began attacking the area of Pakistan. They eventually establish the Delhi Sultanate.
1500s	European traders show interest in goods from the area that would later become Pakistan.
1526	The Delhi Sultanate falls to Mongol (Mughal) forces from central Asia.
1707	The Mughal Empire begins to crumble. British forces gain more power on the Indian subcontinent.
1858	The British government takes control of the Indian subcontinent.
1885	The Indian National Congress is formed to demand an independent India.
1906	Muslim leaders establish the All-India Muslim League, lobbying for an independent Muslim state.
1914	World War I breaks out. Indians hope that aiding the British in the war will lead to independence.
1918	World War I ends. The British refuse to grant India independence.
1919	British soldiers fire on a crowd in Jallianwala Bagh, killing approximately fifteen hundred men, women, and children.
1933	The name Pakistan is first coined.

1939	Britain becomes involved in World War II. Hindus in India refuse to cooperate with the British Empire, but Muslims aid the war effort.
1940	Muslim League officials in British India pass a declaration of independence, demanding an independent Muslim nation.
1945	World War II ends.
1947	The independent nations of India and Pakistan are established.
1965	American immigration laws are changed, allowing more non-European immigrants to enter. The first major wave of Pakistani immigrants comes to America.
1970	Approximately twenty thousand Pakistanis live in America.
1971	East Pakistan declares independence from West Pakistan, and war breaks out. The independent nation of Bangladesh is formed. Pakistanis and Bengalis flee to America to avoid the civil war.
1994	Pakistani Americans begin making major strides in American politics.
2000	An estimated 210,000 Pakistani Americans live in the United States.
2001	Terrorists attack the United States. Some Pakistani Americans become targets of hate crimes and government suspicion. The USA Patriot Act is passed.
2002	Pakistani president General Pervez Musharraf meets with U.S. president George W. Bush to discuss problems facing Pakistani Americans.
2005	The USA Patriot Act comes up for review.

GLOSSARY

CASTE SYSTEM: a rigid social system that separates people based on class. The caste system is practiced by Indian Hindus.

DEPORTATION: the act, usually by the government, of sending immigrants back to their homeland

DETAINEE: a person held by the government for questioning

HINDUISM: a religion founded by Aryans who migrated to India in 500 B.C.

IMMIGRATE: to come to live in a country other than one's homeland. A person who immigrates is called an immigrant.

ISLAM: a religion based on the prophet Muhammad's teachings and founded on the Arabian Peninsula in the seventh century A.D. A person who follows Islam is called a Muslim.

MOSQUE: an Islamic place of worship

PARTITION: the division of India and Pakistan in 1947, when both nations became free of British rule

QURAN: the holy book of Islam. The writings in the Quran were set forth by Muhammad starting in A.D. 610.

REFUGEE: a person forced to flee his or her country due to political upheaval or other danger

THINGS TO SEE AND DO

AMERICAN INSTITUTE OF PAKISTAN STUDIES, PHILADELPHIA, PENNSYLVANIA
http://www.pakistanstudies-aips.org/
This institute is part of the University of Pennsylvania's Middle East Center. It includes information and exhibits about the language, history, and culture of Pakistan, as well as the various ethnic groups living in Pakistan.

EID AL-ADHA, BOSTON, MASSACHUSETTS

Pakistani Americans living in the Boston area celebrate Eid al–Adha, the festival held during the time of pilgrimage to Mecca, with prayers, food, and socializing. Eid al–Adha is also a traditional time to help those in need, so many Pakistani Americans donate food or money to homeless shelters, soup kitchens, and other organizations.

EID AL-FITR, NEW YORK CITY, NEW YORK

America's largest Pakistani American population, Brooklyn's Little Pakistan, celebrates the end of Ramadan, the Muslim month of fasting, with the three–day Eid al–Fitr. The celebration includes special morning prayers, followed by visits to friends and family. The event also features traditional Pakistani cuisine and music, as well as carnival games and stalls selling jewelry, clothing, and perfumes.

LIVING TRADITIONS FESTIVAL, SALT LAKE CITY, UTAH

http://www.slcgov.com/arts/livingtraditions/

This annual festival celebrates the various ethnic groups that make up the Salt Lake City area, including the estimated fifteen hundred Pakistani American families living there. The three–day festival includes dancers, musicians, and cuisine from all over the world, including Pakistan, as well as crafts and workshops.

PAKISTAN INDEPENDENCE DAY PARADE, CHICAGO, ILLINOIS

This annual event takes place August 14 and commemorates the creation of Pakistan in 1947. Pakistani Americans in Chicago celebrate the event with a parade, traditional music, poetry readings, and art exhibits. Community members dressed in traditional Pakistani costumes visit with friends and family.

Source Notes

8   Bapsi Sidhwa, *The Crow Eaters* (Minneapolis: Milkweed Editions, 1992), 48.

19 "South Asian History: The Colonial Legacy in India," *India Resource*, September 17, 2002, http://india_resource.tripod.com/colonial.html (May 3, 2005).

20 "South Asian History: The Two Nation Theory," *India Resource*, August 5, 2003, http://india_resource.tripod.com/hist-2nation.html (May 3, 2005).

34 "Flashback to Indian Partition," *BBC News*, October 25, 2003, http://news.bbc.co.uk/1/hi/world/south_asia/175044.stm (November 15, 2003).

35 "Flashback to Indian Partition."

42 Hina Haq, *Sadika's Way: A Novel of Pakistan and America* (Chicago: Academy Chicago Publishers, 2004), 130.

50 Mark Whittington, "A Dream Deferred No More," *Detroit Free Press–Entertainment*, March 11, 2005, http://ae.freep.com/entertainment/ui/michigan/movie.html?id=268707 (May 2, 2005).

59 Peggy Levitt, "Transnational Options: How Pakistani Immigrants Create Self," paper presented at Culture, Identity, and Inequality Conference, Princeton University, April 2002, http://www.peggylevitt.org/pdfs/4.trans_options.pdf (May 3, 2003).

64 Levitt, 32.

65 Karen Price Hossell, *Pakistani Americans* (Chicago: Heinemann Library, 2004), 9.

SELECTED BIBLIOGRAPHY

The Asian-American Almanac: A Reference Work on Asians in the United States. Detroit: Gale Research, 1995. The almanac looks at the history and culture of Asian Americans, including Pakistanis.

Dworkowitz, Alexander. "Registration Stirs Fears of Queens Pakistanis." *Refuse and Resist!* February 20, 2003. http://www.refuseandresist.org/detentions/art.php?aid=614 (May 1, 2003). This article discusses the fears and obstacles Pakistani immigrants face after the September 11, 2001, terrorist attacks.

"Flashback to Indian Partition," *BBC News,* October 25, 2003, http://news.bbc.co.uk/1/hi/world/south_asia/1757044.stm (November 15, 2003). This article reexamines the events leading up to and the aftermath of partition on the Indian subcontinent.

Hassan, Nasim. "An American Experience." *ContactPakistan.com.* N.d. http://www.contactpakistan.com/Communitylibrary/general/news43.htm (April 20, 2003). Hassan's article covers Pakistani immigration to the United States, focusing on the major wave after 1965 and the demographics of the immigrant group.

Levitt, Peggy. "Transnational Options: How Pakistani Immigrants Create Self." Paper presented at Culture, Identity, and Inequality Conference, Princeton University. April 2002. http://www.peggylevitt.org/pdfs/4.trans_options.pdf (May 3, 2003). This paper explores how Pakistani Americans balance their Pakistani culture with their American home.

Pavri, Tinaz. *Pakistani Americans.* In *Gale Encyclopedia of Multicultural America.* 2nd ed. Detroit: Gale Group, 2000. The article about Pakistan explores the history of Pakistan, immigrant communities in America, and Pakistani American contributions to American culture.

Yusufali, Jabeen. *Pakistan: An Islamic Treasure.* Minneapolis: Dillon Press, 1990. Yusufali discusses the people, history, religion, and culture of Pakistan.

FURTHER READING & WEBSITES

FICTION

English, Karen. *Nadia's Hands.* Honesdale, PA: Boyds Mill Press, 1999. Young Nadia, a Pakistani American girl, learns more about balancing her two worlds on the day of her aunt's wedding.

Shepard, Aaron. *The Gifts of Wali Dad: A Tale of India and Pakistan.* New York: Atheneum Books for Young Readers, 1995. An Indian/Pakistani folktale in which an impoverished glass cutter finds that gifts can be a mixed blessing.

NONFICTION

Ali, Ahmed, ed. *The Golden Tradition: An Anthology of Urdu Poetry.* New York: Columbia University Press, 1973. A collection of Pakistani poems.

Khan, Rukhsana. *Muslim Child: Understanding Islam through Stories and Poems.* Morton Grove, IL: Albert Whitman, 2002. Khan uses stories from eight different people to help non-Muslims understand the essentials of Islam and to highlight the Muslim presence throughout the world.

Martin, Christopher. *Mohandas Gandhi.* Minneapolis: Lerner Publications Company, 2000. This biography covers the life and struggles of the Indian leader Mohandas Gandhi who advocated peace in the fight for Indian independence.

Takai, Ronald. *India in the West: South Asians in America.* New York: Chelsea House Publishers, 1995. While the focus of this book is Indian immigration to America, Takai also discusses other South Asian groups in America, including Pakistanis.

Taus–Bolstad, Stacy. *Pakistan in Pictures.* Minneapolis: Lerner Publications Company, 2003. Learn more about the history, geography, and culture of Pakistan.

WEBSITES

Dawn
http://www.dawn.com
Dawn is Pakistan's most widely

read English-language online
newspaper.

INAMERICABOOKS.COM
http://www.inamericabooks.com
Visit inamericabooks.com, the
online home of the In America
series, to get linked to all sorts of
useful information. You'll find
historical and cultural websites
related to individual groups, as
well as general information on
genealogy, creating your own
family tree, and the history of
immigration in America.

**PAKISTAN AMERICAN CULTURAL
SOCIETY**
http://www.pakistanamericancultur
alsociety.org
The Pakistan American Cultural
Society's website offers
information on upcoming cultural

events in the New York and New
Jersey area.

PAKISTAN LINK
http://www.pakistanlink.com
This is the daily Internet version
of the weekly paper *Pakistan Link*,
published in Los Angeles. The site
offers news stories as well as links
to sports sites, health sites, and
more—all geared toward the
Pakistani American community.

YESPAKISTAN.COM
http://www.yespakistan.com
This site offers links to dozens of
Pakistani American organizations—
cultural, political, and professional.
It also looks at social and political
problems in Pakistan, as well as
giving extra information about the
country's history and people.

INDEX

ACKNOWLEDGMENTS: The photographs in this book are reproduced with the permission of: Digital Vision Royalty Free, pp. 1, 3, 24; © Galen Rowell/CORBIS, p. 6; © Ric Ergenbright/CORBIS, p. 7; © age fotostock/SuperStock, p. 9; © SUHAIB SALEM/Reuters/CORBIS, p. 10; © Maxine Cass, p. 11; The British Library, pp. 14, 16; © Bettmann/CORBIS, pp. 21, 28; Courtesy of the Uppal Family, p. 25; Mary Evans Picture Library, p. 29; © Hulton-Deutsch Collection/CORBIS, p. 30; The Illustrated London News, p. 32; © Hulton|Archive by Getty Images, p. 34; © Spencer Grant, pp. 39, 52; © Rudi Von Briel/PhotoEdit, p. 40; © Joseph Sohm; ChromoSohm Inc./CORBIS, p. 43; © AP/Wide World Photos, pp. 45, 49; © Richard Levine, pp. 46, 47; © Andrew Stawicki/Toronto Star/ZUMA Press, p. 57; © Frances M. Roberts, p. 61; Courtesy of Dr. Mohammed Akhter, p. 66 (left); © Hollywood Book and Poster, p. 66 (right); Helena de la Fontaine © 2005, p. 67; Courtesy of Samina Quraeshi, p. 68; © Robert Holmgren/ZUMA Press, p. 69 (left); Courtesy of Dr. Hassan Zee, p. 69 (right); Maps by Bill Hauser, pp. 33, 50.

Front cover: Digital Vision Royalty Free (title); © SuperStock, Inc./SuperStock (center); Galen Rowell/CORBIS (bottom). Back cover: Digital Vision Royalty Free.